Leonora's m

by Carol Bra

Illustrations by Laura Caiafa

Dedication

To my husband John, my 3 children, their partners and 6 beautiful grandchildren who have encouraged and supported me for the last 10 years through my juicing and clean eating journey. I thank you all, without you it wouldn't have been possible.
There have been many books written on juice and clean eating but mostly aimed at adults so I decided to write for children. After all it is the children who will grow up and hopefully make a difference to the Health and Wellbeing of the generations yet to come. It is time for Leonora!

There is no better place to start than a book. It is where my journey began, and one I am still travelling. Hopefully this will be the first of many, and if it encourages just one child to take an interest in learning about real food and how it helps build a healthy mind and body it will be more than worth it.

The book that changed my life was written by Jason Vale AKA The Juicemaster. Jason has worked tirelessly to promote Juice Therapy around the world. I cannot thank him enough for giving me the opportunity to train at the Juicemaster School of Natural Juice Therapy and become the first qualified Natural Juice Therapist.

Finally, thanks to the lovely Laura Caiafa who has illustrated this story so beautifully, I can't wait to see what you do with our next book about the spring onion called Odhran (Little pale green one).

Copyright ©
Text by Carol Brace
Illustrations by Laura Caiafa
2017

The right of Carol Brace to be identified as the author
and Laura Caiafa to be identified
as the illustrator of this work has been asserted by them in
accordance with the Copyright, Designs and
Patent Act 1988.

All rights reserved. No part of this work may be published or otherwise circulated in any form without the express permission of the authors.

Chapter 1

Leonora was a witch, 10 years old now and still couldn't quite get the hang of exactly what a witch was supposed to do.

Her twin sisters, Luna and Lexi, were very adept at spell casting and although they knew they shouldn't, would cast spells willy-nilly on anyone, just for fun.

It wasn't unusual to see big, red, oozing pustules appear on the faces of anyone within spitting distance of one of their ghastly spells.

They even made old people's hats blow away, then rolled about the floor laughing as they raced after them.

Unlike her sisters, Leonora didn't like being a witch. For as long as she could remember she knew she wasn't like the rest of her family.

She had never cast a spell on anyone, in fact she had never actually learnt how to cast any kind of spell, it just seemed most unkind.

She preferred to think spell casting should be used in a nicer way.

On her way home from school Leonora was thinking about the Easter weekend ahead.

As she turned the corner as usual and walked down Spellbound Avenue there was something exciting in the air, she could feel it.

Leonora loved this way home, especially today, it had been raining earlier but now the sun was shining and everything looked clean and fresh.

The huge trees, beginning to unfurl their leaves looking almost like big, friendly giants.

Smiling, she realised she was thinking out loud.

"Being a witch is horrible, what is a witch anyway? I don't know how to do spells so maybe I'm not a witch at all.

If I was I would want to do something good not make people look hideous, unhappy or trip them up, like Luna and Lexi love to do.

Making things happen like that is just not nice".

Chapter 2

"Why was I was born a witch?"
she said out loud.
"You have already answered your own question, you were born a witch to do some good in the world."

She stopped dead in her tracks as she looked every which way.
The road was empty.

"Who said that, where are you hiding?"

"We did."

"Who is we, and where are you hiding?"

"We are not hiding, we are down here just in front of you, around the roots of the tree."

"All I can see is a pile of empty crisp packets, chocolate wrappers and coke cans."

"We are the packet of spring onion seeds. We were on our way to a nice gentlemen's garden, when those nasty sisters of yours tripped him up and we fell into this pile of rubbish. He was so flustered he missed us."

"Wait a minute, how can I be talking to a packet of spring onion seeds, this is silly, seeds are just seeds, they don't talk."

"Please, just put us in your pocket, take us home and we will explain all."

Leonora picked up the packet and put it in her pocket wishing they were strawberry seeds, then thought, "are strawberries planted as seeds or plants?", anyway it didn't matter, she adored strawberries however they grew, especially with ice cream.

Spring onions, on the other hand didn't fill her with joy at all, in fact they made her scrunch up her face thinking of that oniony smell, no she didn't like spring onions at all.

Reluctantly, she picked them up and put them in her pocket.

She decided not to tell anyone about her interesting find just in case her parents planted them and made her eat them, she disliked the taste of spring onions!

As soon as she arrived home she carefully placed the packet in her special box,
slipped it under the bed,
and went down for tea.

Chapter 3

Mum had made some home made pizza (without onion for Leonora, she disliked onions of any description) with chunky chips made from real potato just as she liked them, followed by a large bowl of banana ice cream, and a few of her favourite strawberries on top.

Leonora excused herself, to finish her homework (she fibbed) and rushed upstairs to her bedroom.

Shutting the door behind her, Leonora turned the key so she wouldn't be disturbed as she pulled her secret box from under the bed.

"Hello, are you there?" she whispered, "I need to ask some questions."

No response.

"Are you there?" she repeated.

Still no response.

She picked up the packet and shook it, there were seeds inside so she hadn't been dreaming.

"You lot are very quiet, why aren't you talking to me?".

Still no answer.

Feeling cross, she threw the packet back in the box, slid it under the bed and went back downstairs joining the others at the table.

Talk of Easter was over, it had been replaced by boring conversation about her sisters' latest escapades.

As soon as there was a lull in conversation Leonora said: "Have any of you ever struck up a conversation with, say, an onion seed?"

The resulting laughter had everyone howling so loud they didn't hear dad come in".
"What's all this then girls, what's the joke?"

"It's Leonora", said Luna and Lexi in unison "she wants to know if anyone has ever spoken to an onion seed," this set them off again, which made Leonora very sad.

"OK girls stop being unkind to your sister." Turning to Leonora dad said.

"That is not such a silly question, your great, great, great, great, grandmother also called Leonora, was known to have powers that far exceeded anything that had been seen before, including the ability to communicate with plants and animals.

Your name Leonora, is always given to the first born girl from generation to generation, and it is her who is said to inherit the "power" which is to be awakened when the world is in need."

Luna and Lexi, with mouths open, lost for words, just stared at Leonora.

Dad kissed Leonora's head as he sat down to eat his tea, "We will talk about this later" he whispered.

Chapter 4

Leonora left the table, walked slowly up to her room and as she slumped on the bed heaved a heavy sigh and said again, **"Why was I born a witch?"**

No sooner had she uttered the words she heard the voices.

She pulled the box from under the bed and lifted the lid.

"I thought I had made it all up, why were you ignoring me, why did you stop talking?"

"That's an easy question to answer.
When we are just seeds and we finish a conversation the power of speech fades as well.

We need to be awakened again by the magic phrase why was I born a witch."

"Oh! I see, I will remember that in future.
So, what happens when you are planted and start to grow?"
"Oh that's easy, when we are growing we can communicate all the time but unfortunately, it is only those with the power who can hear and understand us.

Some of you humans still do talk to us, which makes us very happy and we grow much better, knowing we are loved and appreciated. We are here to feed you so you grow big strong and healthy.

"What did you mean when you said I was born to do some good in the world, what exactly do I have to do?"

"Every so often when the world and its humans are so sick and in need of drastic change, the one with the power is awakened.

You are the one who is able to use very special gifts, one of which is the ability to communicate with plants.

The humans need to be reminded where their food comes from and how we can feed and protect the future generations yet to be born.

You will be taught how to use fruits, vegetables, nuts, seeds and herbs medicinally in the way we were meant to be used.

You will be surprised to know that many little humans today think food comes from the supermarket, we need to get them back into the garden growing, and eating delicious food again.

Your mission, should you choose to accept it, will grow into a lifelong passion.

You will teach the children how to preserve the planet for future generations."

"But how, the planet is such a big place where would I start?"

"You start with us, the spring onion.
Plant us in the vegetable patch and we will teach you all you need to know about what we can do for mankind.

You will then write a book for children about our amazing journey, a book that will amuse and delight them, but will also teach them how we can help them grow big, strong and healthy.

After us you can move on to those strawberries you love so much, we all have our own story to tell, even you humans."

Leonora yawned, she didn't realise how tired she was, she said goodnight to her seeds, put on her pyjamas and cleaned her teeth just before mum and dad came to kiss her goodnight.

Tucked in, Leonora was asleep in no time.

Chapter 5

The next morning the birds seemed to be singing louder than usual which woke Leonora, it was just 6 o'clock so no one else would be awake yet.

Leonora grabbed her dressing gown and the packet of seeds and rushed down the stairs as quickly as she could.

"You're in a hurry today Leonora, where are you going in such a rush?"

"Oh no not again" whispered Leonora, she knew it wasn't the seeds she hadn't woken them up yet.

"Who said that?"

"Its me, my name is Lily, I'm the plant on the side table. You walk past, and ignore me every day on your way to school, I say hello every time you pass so I'm just thrilled you can at last hear me, it's about time someone was sent to sort out our precious planet.

We have been waiting such a long, long time for you!"

"I'm pleased to meet you" said Leonora. "Sorry I can't stop to talk, I have to plant my spring onion seeds to begin my mission, so please excuse me."

"That's ok Leonora, I completely understand, you must be so excited, but I must just tell you that flowers can help you as well, its not just the fruits and vegetables."

"How can flowers help?" asked Leonora.

"Well, like each of you humans, we flowers have our own special "talent" to make the world a much better place.

The problem is, more and more of us have sadly, lost the ability to recognise what our own, special "talent" is."

"Oh how intriguing, but what can you do whilst you are just sitting in your pot inside this house?"

"That's easy, I am one of the plants with a talent for purifying the air, I remove lots of the toxins so you can breathe cleaner air."

Still whispering, Leonora said "How fabulous! thank you so much, I am so glad I got to talk to you, but I really must rush now to plant my seeds before the others get up."

Chapter 6

Leonora quietly opened the back door and stepped into the garden, closing it behind her.

Stop it! I can't hear myself talk!
One at a time please!

Everything went very quiet, then a little ripe strawberry said "At last, the mission has begun, please pick me as your first project".

"If only I could, I love strawberries.
But the spring onions have chosen me, it was these seeds I spoke to first so I need to plant them and wait for them to grow so I can learn all I can to begin my mission.

I promise you will be the next on my list,
I just love strawberries".

"You don't have to wait for them to grow, just cast a spell!"

"Ah, now, that is a problem. I don't know how to cast spells."

Frustrated, the little ripe strawberry said "well you had better learn fast then,
or you will need 2 or 3 lifetimes to complete your mission and our amazing planet can't wait that long!"

"But I don't know how to begin yet!"

"All you need to do is use the spell book,
it is waiting for you in the old greenhouse
which has been hidden at the back of the
garden for years."

"Thank you so much for your help,
I will plant the seeds now and then look for
the book of spells."

Leonora prepared the soil, carefully placing the seeds in neat rows, covering them with another thin layer of soil and finally watered them.

She stood up admiring her handy work, then looked toward the back of the garden.

"Now to find that spell book" she said as she walked toward the back of the garden to find the old greenhouse.

Chapter 7

You couldn't actually see the old greenhouse as it was tucked away in the far corner.

No one ever went to that part of the garden as it was left for the wildlife to enjoy.

She had heard there had been a greenhouse in the corner, but it had not been used since great grandpa had bought the new one, so it must be very rickety now as it was covered with shrubs and bushes, which made it unrecognisable as a greenhouse.

As she reached the corner of the garden, she sighed and said, "How ever am I going to get inside to look for a greenhouse with all those weeds clinging to everything?"

"So you are here at last Leonora, have you any idea how long we have been waiting for you?"

"Hello" said Leonora, not shocked any more when she heard the plants talking.

"My name is Ivy. I've spent many years covering up this greenhouse protecting the spell book for when you arrived to take up your mission. It's not as bad as you think."

As she was speaking the tight web of ivy started to unravel revealing a lovely antique, huge, greenhouse.

As soon as the door was clear Leonora walked in.

It was perfect inside almost as if it were still in use. The windows were clean, as were the tools which hung on hooks just above the bench.

Pots of all different sizes were underneath the bench waiting to be filled with compost for planting.

In the corner was a lovely wooden, beautifully carved box.

Leonora placed her hand on the handle and opened it slowly, revealing a big black, leather bound book with a picture of a big orange pumpkin on the top, the type her and her sisters would carve for their Halloween party each year.

Chapter 8

She removed the book and opened it. It was full of spells on every page, all sorts of spells.

There were even spells that could break spells, this made her smile as she thought of the fun she would have ruining Luna and Lexi's cruel spell casting escapades.

She jumped as dad came through the door. "Here you are, we have been looking everywhere for you, how long have you been out here?"

Leonora turned, "oh dad I have had such an amazing morning, I've made so many new friends.

I have even had a conversation with lily who cleans the air in the house, it is all just so wonderful.

And look at what I have found in great grandpa's greenhouse.

It has been waiting here, just for me, a long, long time.

I have planted the spring onions and now I have to look for the spell to make them grow, because I haven't got time to wait for them to do it themselves because the world has been waiting for a long time and"…

"Whoa, slow down, you have been out here long enough, you need to go in and have your breakfast before you do anymore.

Mum and the girls have gone swimming so you have plenty of time to find your spell after you have eaten.

While you have your breakfast I will put a lock on the box so no one but you can open it.

Now go and eat, get dressed, and come back out when you are ready.

"Thank you dad, I am a bit hungry" she said as she hugged him before running back into the house.

"I'm back" she said bursting through the door of the greenhouse.

Dad gave her the key, excitedly, she opened the box and took out the book, she knew she was going to love reading it, but first she had to find the spell she needed.

It wasn't long before she found it.

She memorised the words, closed the book, put it back in the box, locked it, put the key in her pocket and ran out to where she had planted the spring onions.

Peat and soil
wiggly worms that toil
With sun and rain
bearing down again
Making seeds below
Just grow and grow

As she spoke the words she couldn't quite believe what was happening, the lovely green shoots of the spring onions began to break through the soil.

Almost as soon as she had finished the magical words, the deafening cheers coming from everywhere in the garden didn't stop until every one of those spring onions stood, fully grown swaying in the breeze.

The plants were so happy and pleased, shouts rang out across the garden "You did it Leonora, well done, we are so proud of you." Dad was now by her side looking down at the spring onions.

"Wow, Leonora that is amazing, you have been given a very special gift and I hope now, you know **why you were born a witch**.

You have a very important job to do and I know you will do it well."

Leonora watched him as he walked back to the house, then turned back to the spring onions who said "Right Leonora, you will need your pen and paper, it is time to begin..."